U.S. Department
of Transportation

**Federal Aviation
Administration**

FAA-S-8081-4C

KU-788-541

# INSTRUMENT RATING

## Practical Test Standards

## for

## • AIRPLANE

## • HELICOPTER

## • POWERED LIFT

**OCTOBER 1998**

**FLIGHT STANDARDS SERVICE
Washington, DC 20591**

# INSTRUMENT RATING

## Practical Test Standards

### for

### Airplane

### Helicopter

### Powered Lift

1998

FLIGHT STANDARDS SERVICE
WASHINGTON, DC 20591

## NOTE

Material in FAA-S-8081-4C will be effective October 1,1998. All previous editions of the Instrument Rating Practical Test Standards will be obsolete as of this date.

# FOREWORD

The Instrument Rating Practical Test Standards (PTS) book is published by the Federal Aviation Administration (FAA) to establish the standards for instrument rating certification practical tests for the airplane, helicopter, and powered lift, category and classes. These practical test standards shall also be used for the instrument portion of the commercial pilot airship practical test. FAA inspectors and designated pilot examiners shall conduct practical tests in compliance with these standards. Flight instructors and applicants should find these standards helpful during training and when preparing for practical tests.

---

Richard O. Gordon
Acting Director, Flight Standards Service

# CONTENTS

*FAA-S-8081-4C*

# INTRODUCTION

## General Information

The Flight Standards Service of the Federal Aviation Administration (FAA) has developed this practical test standards book to be used by FAA inspectors and designated pilot examiners when conducting instrument rating—airplane, helicopter, and powered lift practical tests, and instrument proficiency checks for all aircraft. These practical test standards shall also be used for the instrument portion of the commercial pilot–airship practical test. Instructors are expected to use this book when preparing applicants for practical tests. Applicants should be familiar with this book and refer to these standards during their training.

This publication sets forth the practical test requirements for the addition of an instrument rating to a pilot certificate in airplanes, helicopters, and powered-lift aircraft.

Information considered directive in nature is described in this practical test standards book in terms, such as "shall" and "must," indicating the actions are mandatory. Guidance information is described in terms, such as "should" and "may," indicating the actions are desirable or permissive, but not mandatory.

The FAA gratefully acknowledges the valuable assistance provided by many individuals and companies who contributed their time and talent in assisting with the revision of these practical test standards.

These practical test standards may be accessed through the FedWorld Information System by computer modem at 703-321-3339. These standards may also be accessed on the Internet at http://www.fedworld.gov/pub/faa-att/faa-att.htm. This address accesses the index of training and testing files in the FAA-ATT Library on FedWorld. Subsequent changes to these standards, in accordance with AC 60-27, Announcement of Availability: Changes to Practical Test Standards, will be available through FedWorld and then later incorporated into a printed revision. For a listing of changes, AFS-600's Internet web site may be accessed at www.mmac.jccbi.gov/afs/afs600.

This publication may be purchased from the Superintendent of Documents, U.S. Government Printing Office, Washington, DC 20402.

Comments regarding this publication should be sent to:

U.S. Department of Transportation
Federal Aviation Administration
Flight Standards Service
Airman Testing Standards Branch, AFS-630
P.O. Box 25082
Oklahoma City, OK 73125

## Practical Test Standard Concept

Title 14 of the Code of Federal Regulations (14 CFR) part 61 specifies the areas in which knowledge and skill must be demonstrated by the applicant before the issuance of an instrument rating. The CFR's provide the flexibility to permit the FAA to publish practical test standards containing specific TASKS in which pilot competency shall be demonstrated. The FAA will revise this book whenever it is determined that changes are needed in the interest of safety. Adherence to the provisions of the regulations and the practical test standards is mandatory for evaluation of instrument pilot applicants.

## Practical Test Book Description

This test book contains the instrument rating practical test standards for airplane, helicopter, and powered lift. It also contains TASK requirements for the addition of airplane, helicopter, or powered lift, if an instrument rating is possessed by the applicant in at least one other aircraft category. Instrument TASKS for the **commercial pilot–airship** and **instrument proficiency checks** for all aircraft are also contained in these practical test standards.

## Practical Test Standards Description

AREAS OF OPERATION are phases of the practical test arranged in a logical sequence within each standard. They begin with preflight preparation and end with postflight procedures. The examiner may conduct the practical test in any sequence that results in a complete and efficient test.

TASKS are titles of knowledge areas, flight procedures, or maneuvers appropriate to an AREA OF OPERATION.

The applicant who holds an airplane, helicopter, or powered lift instrument rating will not have to take the entire test when applying for an added rating. The TASKS that are required shall be indicated as abbreviated in the following paragraph.

The abbreviations within parentheses immediately following a TASK title indicate whether the TASK is appropriate to airplanes, helicopters, powered lift, airships, instrument proficiency checks, and added ratings. The meaning of the abbreviations follow:

**IA**   Airplane
**AA**   Airplane Added
**A**    Airship
**IH**   Helicopter
**HA**   Helicopter Added
**PC**   Instrument Proficiency Check
**PL**   Powered Lift
**PLA**  Powered Lift Added

A person who does not meet the recent instrument experience requirements of 14 CFR part 61 may not serve as pilot in command under IFR until that person passes an instrument proficiency check. Applicants must successfully complete the TASKS designated as **(PC)** in these practical test standards.

NOTE is used to emphasize special considerations required in the AREA OF OPERATION or TASK.

The REFERENCE identifies the publication(s) that describe(s) the TASK. Descriptions of TASKS are not included in the standards because this information can be found in the current issue of the listed references. Publications other than those listed may be used for references if their content conveys substantially the same meaning as the referenced publications. These practical test standards are based on the following references. The latest revision of these references shall be used.

| | |
|---|---|
| **14 CFR part 61** | Certification: Pilots and Flight Instructors |
| **14 CFR part 91** | General Operating and Flight Rules |
| **AC 00-6** | Aviation Weather |
| **AC 00-45** | Aviation Weather Services |
| **AC 60-28** | English Language Skill Standards Required by 14 CFR parts 61, 63, and 65 |
| **AC 61-21** | Flight Training Handbook |
| **AC 61-23** | Pilot's Handbook of Aeronautical Knowledge |
| **AC 61-27** | Instrument Flying Handbook |
| **AC 61-84** | Role of Preflight Preparation |
| **AC 90-48** | Pilot's Role in Collision Avoidance |
| **AC 90-94** | Guidelines for Using Global Positioning Systems |
| **AIM** | Aeronautical Information Manual |
| **SID's** | Standard Instrument Departures |

*FAA-S-8081-4C*

| STAR's | Standard Terminal Arrivals |
|--------|----------------------------|
| **AFD** | Airport Facility Directory |
| **FDC NOTAM's** | National Flight Data Center Notices to Airmen |
| **IAP** | Instrument Approach Procedures |
| **Others** | Pertinent Pilot's Operating Handbooks |
| | FAA-Approved Flight Manuals |
| | En Route Low Altitude Charts |

The Objective lists the important elements that must be satisfactorily performed to demonstrate competency in a TASK. The Objective includes:

1. specifically what the applicant should be able to do;
2. the conditions under which the TASK is to be performed; and
3. the acceptable standards of performance.

## Use of the Practical Test Standards Book

The instrument rating practical test standards are designed to evaluate competency in both knowledge and skill.

The FAA requires that all practical tests be conducted in accordance with the appropriate practical test standards and the policies set forth in the INTRODUCTION. Instrument rating applicants shall be evaluated in ALL TASKS included in the AREAS OF OPERATION of the appropriate practical test standard (unless instructed or noted otherwise).

In preparation for each practical test, the examiner shall develop a written "plan of action." The "plan of action" shall include all TASKS in each AREA OF OPERATION. If the elements in one TASK have already been evaluated in another TASK, they need not be repeated. For example: the "plan of action" need not include evaluating the applicant on complying with markings, signals, and clearances at the end of the flight if that element was sufficiently observed at the beginning of the flight. Any TASKS selected for evaluation during a practical test shall be evaluated in its entirety.

The TASKS apply to airplanes, helicopters, powered lift, and airships. In certain instances, NOTES describe differences in the performance of a TASK by an "airplane" applicant, "helicopter" applicant, or "powered lift" applicant. When using the practical test standards book, the examiner must evaluate the applicant's knowledge and skill in sufficient depth to determine that the standards of performance listed for all TASKS are met.

All TASKS in these practical test standards are required for the issuance of an instrument rating in airplanes, helicopters, and powered lift. However, when a particular element is not appropriate to the aircraft, its equipment, or operational capability, that element may be omitted. Examples of these element exceptions would be high altitude weather phenomena for helicopters, integrated flight systems for aircraft not so equipped, or other situations where the aircraft or operation is not compatible with the requirement of the element.

The examiner is not required to follow the precise order in which the AREAS OF OPERATION and TASKS appear in this book. The examiner may change the sequence or combine TASKS with similar Objectives to have an orderly and efficient flow of the practical test. For example, emergency descents may be combined with high altitude operations. The examiner's "plan of action" shall include the order and combination of TASKS to be demonstrated by the applicant in a manner that will result in an efficient and valid test.

Examiners shall place special emphasis upon areas of aircraft operation that are most critical to flight safety. Among these are precise aircraft control and sound judgment in Aeronautical Decision Making (ADM). Although these areas may or may not be shown under each TASK, they are essential to flight safety and shall receive careful evaluation throughout the practical test. If these areas are shown in the Objective, additional emphasis shall be placed on them. THE EXAMINER SHALL ALSO EMPHASIZE STALL/SPIN AWARENESS, WAKE TURBULENCE AVOIDANCE, LOW LEVEL WIND SHEAR, COLLISION AVOIDANCE, RUNWAY INCURSION AVOIDANCE, AND CHECKLIST USAGE.

### Practical Test Prerequisites: Instrument Rating

An applicant for an instrument rating practical test is required by 14 CFR part 61 to:

1. hold at least a current private pilot certificate with an aircraft rating appropriate to the instrument rating sought;
2. pass the appropriate instrument rating knowledge test since the beginning of the 24th month before the month in which the practical test is taken;
3. obtain the applicable instruction and aeronautical experience prescribed for the instrument rating sought;
4. hold at least a current third-class medical certificate;
5. be able to read, speak, write, and understand the English language; and

6. obtain a written statement from an authorized flight instructor certifying that the applicant has been given flight instruction in preparation for the practical test within 60 days preceding the date of application. The statement shall also state that the instructor finds the applicant competent to pass the practical test and that the applicant has satisfactory knowledge of the subject area(s) in which a deficiency was indicated by the airman knowledge test report.

If there are questions concerning English language requirements, refer to AC 60-28, English Language Skill Standards Required by 14 CFR parts 61, 63, and 65, or your local Flight Standards District Office (FSDO). English language requirements should be determined to be met prior to beginning the practical test.

## Aircraft and Equipment Required for the Practical Test

The instrument rating applicant is required by 14 CFR part 61 to provide an airworthy, certificated aircraft for use during the practical test. Its operating limitations must not prohibit the TASKS required on the practical test. Flight instruments are those required for controlling the aircraft without outside references. The required radio equipment is that which is necessary for communications with air traffic control (ATC), and for the performance of two of the following nonprecision approaches: (VOR, NDB, GPS, LOC, LDA, SDF) and one precision approach: (glide slope, localizer, marker beacon, and approach lights).

To obtain an **instrument rating with multiengine privileges,** an applicant must demonstrate competency in a multiengine airplane not limited to center thrust. The multiengine airplane that is used to obtain unlimited multiengine privileges must have a $V_{MC}$ speed established by the manufacturer, and produce an asymmetrical thrust configuration with the loss of one or more engines. If an instrument flight test is conducted in a multiengine airplane limited to center thrust, a limitation shall be placed on the applicant's certificate: (INSTRUMENT RATING, AIRPLANE MULTIENGINE, LIMITED TO CENTER THRUST).

When applicants use a single-engine aircraft for the initial instrument practical test, they must complete all the TASKS except the TASKS applying to multiengine aircraft. When applicants use a multiengine aircraft for the initial practical test, they must complete all TASKS including the multiengine TASKS. An applicant with instrument privileges in single-engine aircraft applying for **multiengine instrument privileges** must satisfactorily complete, only: AREA OF OPERATION II (TASKS A, B, and C) and AREA OF OPERATION VII (TASKS B, C, and D).

## Use of FAA-Approved Flight Simulator or Flight Training Device

An airman applicant for instrument rating certification is authorized to use an FAA-qualified and approved flight simulator or flight training device, to complete certain flight TASK requirements listed in this practical test standard.

When flight TASKS are accomplished in an aircraft, certain TASK elements may be accomplished through "simulated" actions in the interest of safety and practicality, but when accomplished in a flight simulator or flight training device, these same actions would not be "simulated." For example, when in an aircraft, a simulated engine fire may be addressed by retarding the throttle to idle, simulating the shutdown of the engine, simulating the discharge of the fire suppression agent, if applicable, simulating the disconnect of associated electrical, hydraulic, and pneumatics systems, etc. However, when the same emergency condition is addressed in a flight simulator or flight training device, all TASK elements must be accomplished as would be expected under actual circumstances.

Similarly, safety of flight precautions taken in the aircraft for the accomplishment of a specific maneuver or procedure (such as limiting altitude in an approach to stall or setting maximum airspeed for an engine failure expected to result in a rejected takeoff) need not be taken when a flight simulator or flight training device is used.

It is important to understand that whether accomplished in an aircraft, flight simulator or flight training device, all TASKS and elements for each maneuver or procedure shall have the same performance standards applied equally for determination of overall satisfactory performance.

The applicant must demonstrate all of the instrument approach procedures required by 14 CFR part 61. At least one instrument approach procedure must be demonstrated in an airplane, helicopter, or powered lift as appropriate. At least one precision and one nonprecision approach not selected for actual flight demonstration may be performed in flight simulators or flight training devices that meet the requirements of appendix 1 of this practical test standard.

## Examiner[1] Responsibility

The examiner conducting the practical test is responsible for determining that the applicant meets the acceptable standards of knowledge and skill of each TASK within the appropriate practical test standard. Since there is no formal division between the "oral" and "skill" portions of the practical test, this becomes an ongoing process throughout the test. To avoid unnecessary distractions, oral questioning should be used judiciously at all times, especially during the flight portion of the practical test.

Examiners shall test to the greatest extent practicable the applicant's correlative abilities rather than mere rote enumeration of facts throughout the practical test.

During the flight portion of the practical test, the examiner shall evaluate the applicant's use of visual scanning, and collision avoidance procedures, when appropriate. Except for takeoff and landing, all TASKS shall be conducted solely by reference to instruments under actual or simulated instrument flight conditions.

The examiner may not assist the applicant in the management of the aircraft, radio communications, navigational equipment, and navigational charts. In the event the test is conducted in an aircraft operation requiring a crew of two, the examiner may assume the duties of the second in command. Most helicopters certified for IFR operations must be flown using two pilots or a single pilot with an approved autopilot or a stability augmentation system (SAS). Therefore, when conducting practical tests in a helicopter (without autopilot, SAS, or copilot), examiners may act as an autopilot (e.g., hold heading and altitude), when requested, to allow applicants to tune radios, select charts, etc. Examiners may perform the same functions as an autopilot but should not act as a copilot performing more extensive duties. The examiner shall remain alert for other traffic at all times. The examiner shall use proper ATC terminology when simulating ATC clearances.

## Satisfactory Performance

Satisfactory performance to meet the requirements for certification is based on the applicant's ability to safely:

1.  perform the approved AREAS OF OPERATION for the certificate or rating sought within the approved standards;

---

[1] The word "examiner" is used throughout the standard to denote either the FAA inspector or FAA designated pilot examiner who conducts an official practical test.

2. demonstrate mastery of the aircraft with the successful outcome of each TASK performed never seriously in doubt;
3. demonstrate satisfactory proficiency and competency within the approved standards;
4. demonstrate sound judgment and ADM; and
5. demonstrate single-pilot competence if the aircraft is type certificated for single-pilot operations.

## Unsatisfactory Performance

If, in the judgment of the examiner, the applicant does not meet the standards of performance of any TASK performed, the associated AREA OF OPERATION is failed and therefore, the practical test is failed. The examiner or applicant may discontinue the test at any time after the failure of an AREA OF OPERATION which makes the applicant ineligible for the certificate or rating sought. The test will be continued only with the consent of the applicant. If the test is either continued or discontinued, the applicant is entitled to credit for only those AREAS OF OPERATION satisfactorily performed. However, during the retest and at the discretion of the examiner, any TASK may be reevaluated including those previously passed.

Typical areas of unsatisfactory performance and grounds for disqualification are:

1. Any action or lack of action by the applicant that requires corrective intervention by the examiner to maintain safe flight.
2. Failure to use proper and effective visual scanning techniques, when applicable, to clear the area before and while performing maneuvers.
3. Consistently exceeding tolerances stated in the Objectives.
4. Failure to take prompt corrective action when tolerances are exceeded.

When a disapproval notice is issued, the examiner shall record the applicant's unsatisfactory performance in terms of AREA OF OPERATIONS appropriate to the practical test conducted.

## Letter of Discontinuance

When a practical test is discontinued for reasons other than unsatisfactory performance (i.e., equipment failure, weather, illness), FAA Form 8710.1, Airman Certificate and/or Rating Application, and, if applicable, AC Form 8080-2, Airman Knowledge Test Report, shall be returned to the applicant. The examiner at that time should prepare, sign, and issue a Letter of Discontinuance to the applicant. The Letter of Discontinuance should identify the AREAS OF OPERATION of the practical test that were successfully completed. The applicant shall be advised that the Letter of Discontinuance shall be presented to the examiner when the practical test is resumed, and made part of the certification file.

## Crew Resource Management (CRM)

CRM " ...refers to the effective use of ALL available resources; human resources, hardware, and information." Human resources "...includes all other groups routinely working with the cockpit crew (or pilot) who are involved in decisions that are required to operate a flight safely. These groups include, but are not limited to: dispatchers, cabin crewmembers, maintenance personnel, and air traffic controllers." CRM is not a single TASK, it is a set of skill competencies that must be evident in all TASKS in this practical test standard as applied to either single pilot or a crew operation. Examiners are required to exercise proper CRM competencies in conducting tests as well as expecting the same from applicants.

## Applicant's Use of Checklists

Throughout the practical test, the applicant is evaluated on the use of an appropriate checklist. Proper use is dependent on the specific TASK being evaluated. The situation may be such that the use of the checklist, while accomplishing elements of an Objective, would be either unsafe or unfeasible, especially in a single-pilot operation. In this case, the method might demand the need to review the checklist after the elements have been met. In any case, use of a checklist must consider proper scanning vigilance and division of attention at all times.

## Use of Distractions During Practical Tests

Numerous studies indicate that many accidents have occurred when the pilot has been distracted during critical phases of flight. To evaluate the pilot's ability to utilize proper control technique while dividing attention both inside and outside the cockpit, the examiner shall cause a realistic distraction during the flight portion of the practical test to evaluate the applicant's ability to divide attention while maintaining safe flight.

## Metric Conversion Initiative

To assist the pilots in understanding and using the metric measurement system, the practical test standards refer to the metric equivalent of various altitudes throughout. The inclusion of meters is intended to familiarize pilots with its use. The metric altimeter is arranged in 10 meter increments; therefore, when converting from feet to meters, the exact conversion, being too exact for practical purposes, is rounded to the nearest 10 meter increment or even altitude as necessary.

## Positive Exchange of Flight Controls

During flight, there must always be a clear understanding between pilots of who has control of the aircraft. Prior to flight, a briefing should be conducted that includes the procedure for the exchange of flight controls. A positive three-step process in the exchange of flight controls between pilots is a proven procedure and one that is strongly recommended.

When one pilot wishes to give the other pilot control of the aircraft, he or she will say "You have the flight controls." The other pilot acknowledges immediately by saying, "I have the flight controls." The first pilot again says "You have the flight controls." When control is returned to the first pilot, follow the same procedure. A visual check is recommended to verify that the exchange has occurred. There should never be any doubt as to who is flying the aircraft.

## Flight Instructor Responsibility

An appropriately rated flight instructor is responsible for training the instrument rating pilot applicant to acceptable standards in all subject matter areas, procedures, and maneuvers included in the TASKS within the appropriate instrument rating pilot practical test standard. Because of the impact of their teaching activities in developing safe, proficient pilots, flight instructors should exhibit a high level of knowledge, skill, and the ability to impart that knowledge and skill to students. Additionally, the flight instructor must certify that the applicant is able to perform safely as an instrument pilot and is competent to pass the required practical test.

Throughout the applicant's training, the flight instructor is responsible for emphasizing the performance of effective visual scanning, collision avoidance, and runway incursion avoidance procedures. These areas are covered, in part, in AC 90-48, Pilot's Role in Collision Avoidance; AC 61-21, Flight Training Handbook; AC 61-23, Pilot's Handbook of Aeronautical Knowledge; and the Aeronautical Information Manual.

## Emphasis on Attitude Instrument Flying and Partial-Panel Skills

The FAA is concerned about numerous fatal aircraft accidents involving spatial disorientation of instrument-rated pilots who have attempted to control and maneuver their aircraft in clouds with inoperative gyroscopic heading and attitude indicators.

Many of the light aircraft operated in instrument meteorological conditions (IMC) are not equipped with dual, independent, gyroscopic heading or attitude indicators and in many cases are equipped with only a single-vacuum source. Therefore, the FAA has stressed that it is imperative for instrument pilots to acquire and maintain adequate partial-panel instrument skills and that they be cautioned not to be overly reliant upon the gyro-instrument systems.

The instrument rating practical test standards place increased emphasis on basic attitude instrument flying and require the demonstration of partial-panel, nonprecision instrument approach procedures.

Applicants may have an unfair advantage during partial-panel TASKS during an instrument approach due to the location of the magnetic compass in some aircraft. When cross-checking the magnetic compass heading, a view of the runway or other visual clue may be sighted. It is the examiner's responsibility to determine if the applicant is receiving visual clues from outside the cockpit. If an examiner feels that the applicant is receiving outside visual clues, the examiner may devise other options to limit the applicant's view. By no means shall the examiner limit his or her view as the safety pilot.

AREA OF OPERATION IV requires the performance of basic instrument flight TASKS under both full-panel and partial-panel conditions. These TASKS are described in detail in AC 61-27, Instrument Flying Handbook. The TASKS require a knowledge of attitude instrument flying procedures and a demonstration of the skills to perform the basic instrument maneuvers with full-instrument-panel and with certain instruments inoperative. The attitude instrument flying system of teaching is described in AC 61-27 and is recommended by the FAA because it requires specific knowledge and interpretation of each individual instrument during training. The Instrument Flight Instructor Lesson Guide in AC 61-27 also provides a course of training which is designed to develop the student's partial-panel skills.

A nonprecision partial-panel approach is considered one of the most demanding situations that could be encountered. If applicants can master this situation, they can successfully complete a less difficult precision approach. **If an actual partial-panel approach in IMC becomes necessary, a less difficult precision approach should be requested, if available. Sound judgment would normally dictate such requests. However, this TASK during the instrument practical test requires that a nonprecision approach be performed.**

Examiners should determine that the applicant demonstrates competency in either the PRIMARY and SUPPORTING or the CONTROL and PERFORMANCE CONCEPT method of instrument flying.

# CONTENTS

# APPLICANT'S PRACTICAL TEST CHECKLIST

## APPOINTMENT WITH EXAMINER:

**EXAMINER'S NAME**_____

**LOCATION** _____

**DATE/TIME** _____

### ACCEPTABLE AIRCRAFT

- ☐ View-limiting device
- ☐ Aircraft Documents: Airworthiness Certificate
- ☐ Registration Certificate
- ☐ Rating Limitations
- ☐ Aircraft Maintenance Records: Airworthiness Inspections

### PERSONAL EQUIPMENT

- ☐ Current Aeronautical Charts
- ☐ Computer and Plotter
- ☐ Flight Plan Form
- ☐ Flight Logs
- ☐ Current AIM

### PERSONAL RECORDS

- ☐ Identification - Photo/Signature ID
- ☐ Pilot Certificate
- ☐ Medical Certificate
- ☐ Completed FAA Form 8710-1, Application for an Airman Certificate and/or Rating
- ☐ Airman Knowledge Test Report
- ☐ Logbook with Instructor's Endorsement
- ☐ Notice of Disapproval (if applicable)
- ☐ Approved School Graduation Certificate (if applicable)
- ☐ Examiner's Fee (if applicable)

*FAA-S-8081-4C*

# EXAMINER'S PRACTICAL TEST CHECKLIST

## AIRCRAFT (IA, IH, PL, A, AA, HA, PLA)

**APPLICANT'S NAME**_____

**LOCATION**_____

**DATE/TIME**_____

## I. PREFLIGHT PREPARATION

☐ **A.** Weather Information (IA, IH, PL, A)
☐ **B.** Cross-Country Flight Planning (IA, IH, PL, A)

## II. PREFLIGHT PROCEDURES

☐ **A.** Aircraft Systems Related to IFR Operations (IA, IH, PL, A, AA, HA, PLA, PC)
☐ **B.** Aircraft Flight Instruments and Navigation Equipment (IA, IH, PL, A, PC)
☐ **C.** Instrument Cockpit Check (IA, IH, PL, A, AA, HA, PLA, PC)

## III. AIR TRAFFIC CONTROL CLEARANCES AND PROCEDURES

☐ **A.** Air Traffic Control Clearances (IA,IH, PL, A, PC)
☐ **B.** Compliance with Departure, En Route, and Arrival Procedures and Clearances (IA, IH, PL, A, PC)
☐ **C.** Holding Procedures (IA, IH, PL, A, PC)

## IV. FLIGHT BY REFERENCE TO INSTRUMENTS

☐ **A.** Straight-and-Level Flight (IA, IH, PL, AA, HA, PLA, PC)
☐ **B.** Change of Airspeed ( IA, IH, PL, AA, HA, PLA, PC)
☐ **C.** Constant Airspeed Climbs and Descents (IA, IH, PL, AA, HA, PLA, PC)
☐ **D.** Rate Climbs and Descents (IA, IH, PL, AA HA, PLA)
☐ **E.** Timed Turns to Magnetic Compass Headings IA, IH, PL)
☐ **F.** Steep Turns (IA, IH, PL, AA, HA, PLA)
☐ **G.** Recovery from Unusual Flight Attitudes(IA, IH, PL, AA, HA, PLA, PC)

## V. NAVIGATION SYSTEMS

☐　Intercepting and Tracking Navigational Systems and DME Arcs (IA, IH, PL, A, PC)

## VI. INSTRUMENT APPROACH PROCEDURES

☐ **A.** Nonprecision Instrument Approach (IA, IH, PL, A, AA, HA, PLA, PC)
☐ **B.** Precision ILS Instrument Approach (IA, IH, PL, A, AA, HA, PLA, PC)
☐ **C.** Missed Approach (IA, IH, PL, A, AA, HA, PLA, PC)
☐ **D.** Circling Approach (IA, A, AA)
☐ **E.** Landing from a Straight-in or Circling Approach (IA, IH, PL, AA, HA, PLA)

## VII. EMERGENCY OPERATIONS

☐ **A.** Loss of Communications (IA, IH, PL, A)
☐ **B.** One Engine Inoperative During Straight-and-Level Flight and Turns **(Multiengine)** (IA, IH, PL, A, AA, HA, PLA, PC)
☐ **C.** One Engine Inoperative Instrument Approach   **(Multiengine)** (IA, IH, PL, A, AA, PLA, PC)
☐ **D.** Loss of Gyro Attitude and/or Heading Indicators (IA, IH, PL)

## VIII.　POSTFLIGHT PROCEDURES

☐　Checking Instruments and Equipment (IA, IH, PL, A, AA, HA, PLA)

# I. AREA OF OPERATION:
## PREFLIGHT PREPARATION

### A. TASK: WEATHER INFORMATION (IA, IH, PL, A)

REFERENCES: 14 CFR part 61; AC 00-6, AC 00-45; AIM.

**NOTE:** Where current weather reports, forecasts, or other pertinent information is not available, this information will be simulated by the examiner in a manner which will adequately measure the applicant's competence.

**Objective.** To determine that the applicant:

1. Exhibits adequate knowledge of the elements related to aviation weather information by obtaining, reading, and analyzing the applicable items, such as

   a. weather reports and forecasts.
   b. pilot and radar reports.
   c. surface analysis charts.
   d. radar summary charts.
   e. significant weather prognostics.
   f. winds and temperatures aloft.
   g. freezing level charts.
   h. stability charts.
   i. severe weather outlook charts.
   j. tables and conversion graphs.
   k. SIGMET s and AIRMET s.
   l. ATIS reports.

2. Correctly analyzes the assembled weather information pertaining to the proposed route of flight and destination airport, and determines whether an alternate airport is required, and, if required, whether the selected alternate airport meets the regulatory requirement.

## B. TASK: CROSS-COUNTRY FLIGHT PLANNING (IA, IH, PL, A)

REFERENCES: 14 CFR parts 61, 91; AC 61-27, AC 61-23, AC 90-94; AFD; AIM.

**Objective.** To determine that the applicant:

1.  Exhibits adequate knowledge of the elements by presenting and explaining a preplanned cross-country flight, as previously assigned by the examiner (preplanning is at examiner s discretion). It should be planned using real time weather and conform to the regulatory requirements for instrument flight rules within the airspace in which the flight will be conducted.

2.  Exhibits adequate knowledge of the aircraft's performance capabilities by calculating the estimated time en route and total fuel requirement based upon factors, such as

    a.  power settings.
    b.  operating altitude or flight level.
    c.  wind.
    d.  fuel reserve requirements.

3.  Selects and correctly interprets the current and applicable en route charts, Standard Instrument Departure (SID), Standard Terminal Arrival (STAR), and Standard Instrument Approach Procedure Charts (IAP).

4.  Obtains and correctly interprets applicable NOTAM information.

5.  Determines the calculated performance is within the aircraft's capability and operating limitations.

6.  Completes and files a flight plan in a manner that accurately reflects the conditions of the proposed flight. (Does not have to be filed with ATC.)

7.  Demonstrates adequate knowledge of Global Positioning Systems (GPS) and Receiver Autonomous Integrity Monitoring (RAIM) capability, when aircraft is so equipped.

## II. AREA OF OPERATION:
## PREFLIGHT PROCEDURES

### A. TASK: AIRCRAFT SYSTEMS RELATED TO IFR OPERATIONS (IA, IH, PL, A, PC)

REFERENCES: 14 CFR parts 61, 91; AC 61-27, AC 61-84.

**Objective.** To determine that the applicant exhibits adequate knowledge of the elements related to applicable aircraft anti-icing/deicing system(s) and their operating methods to include:

1. Airframe.
2. Propeller/intake.
3. Fuel.
4. Pitot-static.

### B. TASK: AIRCRAFT FLIGHT INSTRUMENTS AND NAVIGATION EQUIPMENT (IA, IH, PL, A, PC)

REFERENCES: 14 CFR parts 61, 91; AC 61-27, AC 61-84, AC 90-48.

**Objective.** To determine that the applicant:

1. Exhibits adequate knowledge of the elements related to applicable aircraft flight instrument system(s) and their operating characteristics to include

    a. pitot-static.
    b. altimeter.
    c. airspeed indicator.
    d. vertical speed indicator.
    e. attitude indicator.
    f. horizontal situation indicator.
    g. magnetic compass.
    h. turn-and-slip indicator/turn coordinator.
    i. heading indicator.
    j. electrical systems.
    k. vacuum systems.

2. Exhibits adequate knowledge of the applicable aircraft navigation system(s) and their operating characteristics to include

    a. VHF omnirange (VOR).
    b. distance measuring equipment (DME).
    c. instrument landing system (ILS).
    d. marker beacon receiver/indicators.

e.   transponder/altitude encoding.
f.    automatic direction finder (ADF).
g.   global positioning system (GPS)

## C. TASK:   INSTRUMENT COCKPIT CHECK (IA, IH, PL, A, PC)

REFERENCES: 14 CFR parts 61, 91; AC 61-27.

**Objective.**   To determine that the applicant:

1.   Exhibits adequate knowledge of the elements related to preflighting instruments, avionics, and navigation equipment cockpit check by explaining the reasons for the check and how to detect possible defects.
2.   Performs the preflight on instruments, avionics, and navigation equipment cockpit check by following the checklist appropriate to the aircraft flown.
3.   Determines that the aircraft is in condition for safe instrument flight including

    a.   radio communications equipment.
    b.   radio navigation equipment including the following, as appropriate to the aircraft flown:

        (1)   VOR/VORTAC.
        (2)   ADF.
        (3)   ILS.
        (4)   GPS.
        (5)   LORAN.

    c.   magnetic compass.
    d.   heading indicator.
    e.   attitude indicator.
    f.   altimeter.
    g.   turn-and-slip indicator/turn coordinator.
    h.   vertical speed indicator.
    i.   airspeed indicator.
    j.   clock.
    k.   power source for gyro-instruments.
    l.   pitot heat.

4.   Notes any discrepancies and determines whether the aircraft is safe for instrument flight or requires maintenance.

## III. AREA OF OPERATION:
## AIR TRAFFIC CONTROL CLEARANCES AND PROCEDURES

**NOTE**: The ATC clearance may be an actual or simulated ATC clearance based upon the flight plan.

### A. TASK: AIR TRAFFIC CONTROL CLEARANCES(IA, IH, PL, A, PC)

REFERENCES: 14 CFR parts 61, 91; AC 61-27; AIM.

**Objective.** To determine that the applicant:

1. Exhibits adequate knowledge of the elements related to ATC clearances and pilot/controller responsibilities to include tower en route control and clearance void times.
2. Copies correctly, in a timely manner, the ATC clearance as issued.
3. Determines that it is possible to comply with ATC clearance.
4. Interprets correctly the ATC clearance received and, when necessary, requests clarification, verification, or change.
5. Reads back correctly, in a timely manner, the ATC clearance in the sequence received.
6. Uses standard phraseology when reading back clearance.
7. Sets the appropriate communication and navigation frequencies and transponder codes in compliance with the ATC clearance.

### B. TASK: COMPLIANCE WITH DEPARTURE, EN ROUTE, AND ARRIVAL PROCEDURES AND CLEARANCES (IA, IH, PL, A, PC)

REFERENCES: 14 CFR parts 61, 91; AC 61-27; SID s; En Route Low Altitude Charts; STAR s.

**Objective.** To determine that the applicant:

1. Exhibits adequate knowledge of the elements related to SID s, IFR departure procedures, En Route Low Altitude Charts, STAR s, and related pilot/controller responsibilities.
2. Uses the current and appropriate navigation publications for the proposed flight.
3. Selects and uses the appropriate communication frequencies; selects and identifies the navigation aids associated with the proposed flight.
4. Performs the appropriate aircraft checklist items relative to the phase of flight.
5. Establishes two-way communications with the proper controlling agency, using proper phraseology.

*FAA-S-8081-4C*

6.  Complies, in a timely manner, with all ATC instructions and airspace restrictions.
7.  Exhibits adequate knowledge of two-way radio communication failure procedures.
8.  Intercepts, in a timely manner, all courses, radials, and bearings appropriate to the procedure, route, or clearance.
9.  Maintains the applicable airspeed within 10 knots; headings within 10 ; altitude within 100 feet (30 meters); and tracks a course, radial, or bearing.

## C. TASK: HOLDING PROCEDURES (IA, IH, PL, A, PC)

REFERENCES: 14 CFR parts 61, 91; AC 61-27; AIM.

**NOTE:** Any reference to DME will be disregarded if the aircraft is not so equipped.

**Objective.** To determine that the applicant:

1.  Exhibits adequate knowledge of the elements related to holding procedures.
2.  Changes to the holding airspeed appropriate for the altitude or aircraft when 3 minutes or less from, but prior to arriving at, the holding fix.
3.  Explains and uses an entry procedure that ensures the aircraft remains within the holding pattern airspace for a standard, nonstandard, published, or nonpublished holding pattern.
4.  Recognizes arrival at the holding fix and initiates prompt entry into the holding pattern.
5.  Complies with ATC reporting requirements.
6.  Uses the proper timing criteria, where applicable, as required by altitude or ATC instructions.
7.  Complies with pattern leg lengths when a DME distance is specified.
8.  Uses proper wind correction procedures to maintain the desired pattern and to arrive over the fix as close as possible to a specified time.
9.  Maintains the airspeed within 10 knots; altitude within 100 feet (30 meters); headings within 10 ; and tracks a selected course, radial, or bearing.

## IV. AREA OF OPERATION:
## FLIGHT BY REFERENCE TO INSTRUMENTS

**NOTE:** The examiner shall require the performance of all TASKS. At least two of the TASKS, A through E as selected by the examiner, shall be performed without the use of the attitude and heading indicators. TASK F shall be performed using all available instruments; TASK G shall be performed without the use of the attitude indicator.

### A. TASK: STRAIGHT-AND-LEVEL FLIGHT (IA, IH, PL, AA, HA, PLA, PC)

REFERENCES: 14 CFR part 61; AC 61-27.

**Objective.** To determine that the applicant:

1. Exhibits adequate knowledge of the elements related to attitude instrument flying during straight-and-level flight.
2. Maintains straight-and-level flight in the aircraft configuration specified by the examiner.
3. Maintains the heading within 10 , altitude within 100 feet (30 meters), and airspeed within 10 knots.
4. Uses proper instrument cross-check and interpretation, and applies the appropriate pitch, bank, power, and trim corrections.

### B. TASK: CHANGE OF AIRSPEED (IA, IH, PL, AA, HA, PLA, PC)

REFERENCES: 14 CFR part 61; AC 61-27.

**Objective.** To determine that the applicant:

1. Exhibits adequate knowledge of the elements relating to attitude instrument flying during change of airspeeds in straight-and-level flight and in turns.
2. Establishes a proper power setting when changing airspeed.
3. Maintains the heading within 10 , angle of bank within 5 when turning, altitude within 100 feet (30 meters), and airspeed within 10 knots.
4. Uses proper instrument cross-check and interpretation, and applies the appropriate pitch, bank, power, and trim corrections.

# C. TASK: CONSTANT AIRSPEED CLIMBS AND DESCENTS (IA, IH, PL, A, AA, HA, PLA)

REFERENCES: 14 CFR part 61; AC 61-27.

**Objective.** To determine that the applicant:

1. Exhibits adequate knowledge of the elements relating to attitude instrument flying during constant airspeed climbs and descents.
2. Demonstrates climbs and descents at a constant airspeed between specific altitudes in straight or turning flight as specified by the examiner.
3. Enters constant airspeed climbs and descents from a specified altitude, airspeed, and heading.
4. Establishes the appropriate change of pitch and power to establish the desired climb and descent performance.
5. Maintains the airspeed within 10 knots, heading within 10 or, if in a turning maneuver, within 5 of the specified bank angle.
6. Performs the level-off within 100 feet (30 meters) of the specified altitude.
7. Uses proper instrument cross-check and interpretation, and applies the appropriate pitch, bank, power, and trim corrections.

# D. TASK: RATE CLIMBS AND DESCENTS (IA, IH, PL, AA, HA, PLA)

REFERENCES: 14 CFR part 61; AC 61-27.

**Objective.** To determine that the applicant:

1. Exhibits adequate knowledge of the elements relating to attitude instrument flying during rate climbs and descents.
2. Demonstrates climbs and descents at a constant rate between specific altitudes in straight or turning flight as specified by the examiner.
3. Enters rate climbs and descents from a specified altitude, airspeed, and heading.
4. Establishes the appropriate change of pitch, bank, and power to establish the specified rate of climb or descent.
5. Maintains the specified rate of climb and descent within 100 feet per minute, airspeed within 10 knots, heading within 10 , or if in a turning maneuver, within 5 of the specified bank angle.

6. Performs the level-off within 100 feet (30 meters) of the specified altitude.
7. Uses proper instrument cross-check and interpretation, and applies the appropriate pitch, bank, power, and trim corrections.

## E. TASK: TIMED TURNS TO MAGNETIC COMPASS HEADINGS (IA, IH, PL)

REFERENCES: 14 CFR part 61; AC 61-27.

**NOTE:** If the aircraft has a turn and slip indicator, the phrase miniature aircraft of the turn coordinator applies to the turn needle.

**Objective.** To determine that the applicant:

1. Exhibits adequate knowledge of elements and procedures relating to calibrating the miniature aircraft of the turn coordinator, the operating characteristics and errors of the magnetic compass, and the performance of timed turns to specified compass headings.
2. Establishes indicated standard rate turns, both right and left.
3. Applies the clock correctly to the calibration procedure.
4. Changes the miniature aircraft position, as necessary, to produce a standard rate turn.
5. Makes timed turns to specified compass headings.
6. Maintains the altitude within 100 feet (30 meters), airspeed within 10 knots, bank angle 5 of a standard or half-standard rate turn, and rolls out on specified headings within 10 .

## F. TASK: STEEP TURNS (IA, IH, PL, AA, HA, PLA)

REFERENCES: 14 CFR part 61; AC 61-27.

**Objective.** To determine that the applicant:

1. Exhibits adequate knowledge of the factors relating to attitude instrument flying during steep turns.
2. Enters a turn using a bank of approximately 45 for an airplane and 30 for a helicopter.
3. Maintains the specified angle of bank for either 180 or 360 of turn, both left and right.
4. Maintains altitude within 100 feet (30 meters), airspeed within 10 knots, 5 of specified bank angle, and rolls out within 10 of the specified heading.
5. Uses proper instrument cross-check and interpretation, and applies the appropriate pitch, bank, power, and trim corrections.

# G. TASK: RECOVERY FROM UNUSUAL FLIGHT ATTITUDES (IA, IH, PL, AA, HA, PLA, PC)

REFERENCES: 14 CFR part 61; AC 61-27.

**NOTE:** Any intervention by the examiner to prevent the aircraft from exceeding any operating limitations, or entering an unsafe flight condition, shall be disqualifying.

**Objective.** To determine that the applicant:

1. Exhibits adequate knowledge of the elements relating to attitude instrument flying during recovery from unusual flight attitudes (both nose-high and nose-low).
2. Uses proper instrument cross-check and interpretation, and applies the appropriate pitch, bank, and power corrections in the correct sequence to return the aircraft to a stabilized level flight attitude.

# V. AREA OF OPERATION:
## NAVIGATION SYSTEMS

**TASK:** INTERCEPTING AND TRACKING NAVIGATIONAL SYSTEMS AND DME ARCS (IA, IH, PL, A, PC)

REFERENCES: 14 CFR parts 61, 91; AC 61-27; AIM.

**NOTE:** Any reference to DME arcs, ADF, or GPS shall be disregarded if the aircraft is not equipped with these specified navigational systems.

**Objective.** To determine that the applicant:

1. Exhibits adequate knowledge of the elements related to intercepting and tracking navigational systems and DME arcs.
2. Tunes and correctly identifies the navigation facility.
3. Sets and correctly orients the radial to be intercepted into the course selector or correctly identifies the radial on the RMI.
4. Intercepts the specified radial at a predetermined angle, inbound or outbound from a navigational facility.
5. Maintains the airspeed within 10 knots, altitude within 100 feet (30 meters), and selected headings within 5 .
6. Applies proper correction to maintain a radial, allowing no more than three-quarter-scale deflection of the CDI or within 10 in case of an RMI.
7. Determines the aircraft position relative to the navigational facility or from a waypoint in the case of GPS.
8. Intercepts a DME arc and maintains that arc within 1 nautical mile.
9. Recognizes navigational receiver or facility failure, and when required, reports the failure to ATC.

## VI. AREA OF OPERATION:
## INSTRUMENT APPROACH PROCEDURES

### A. TASK: NONPRECISION INSTRUMENT APPROACH (IA, IH, PL, A, AA, HA, PLA, PC)

REFERENCES: 14 CFR parts 61, 91; AC 61-27; IAP; AIM.

**NOTE:** Any reference to DME arcs, ADF, or GPS shall be disregarded if the aircraft is not equipped with the above specified navigational systems. If the aircraft is equipped with any of the above navigational systems, the examiner may ask the applicant to demonstrate those types of approaches. The examiner shall select two nonprecision approaches utilizing different approach systems.

**Objective.** To determine that the applicant:

1. Exhibits adequate knowledge of the elements related to an instrument approach procedure.
2. Selects and complies with the appropriate instrument approach procedure to be performed.
3. Establishes two-way communications with ATC, as appropriate, to the phase of flight or approach segment, and uses proper radio communication phraseology and technique.
4. Selects, tunes, identifies, and confirms the operational status of navigation equipment to be used for the approach procedure.
5. Complies with all clearances issued by ATC or the examiner.
6. Recognizes if heading indicator and/or attitude indicator is inaccurate or inoperative, advises controller, and proceeds with approach.
7. Advises ATC or examiner anytime the aircraft is unable to comply with a clearance.
8. Establishes the appropriate aircraft configuration and airspeed considering turbulence and wind shear, and completes the aircraft checklist items appropriate to the phase of the flight.
9. Maintains, prior to beginning the final approach segment, altitude within 100 feet (30 meters), heading within 10 and allows less than a full-scale deflection of the CDI or within 10 in the case of an RMI, and maintains airspeed within 10 knots.

10.    Applies the necessary adjustments to the published MDA and visibility criteria for the aircraft approach category when required, such as

    a.    FDC and Class II NOTAM s.
    b.    inoperative aircraft and ground navigation equipment.
    c.    inoperative visual aids associated with the landing environment.
    d.    National Weather Service (NWS) reporting factors and criteria.

11.    Establishes a rate of descent and track that will ensure arrival at the MDA prior to reaching the MAP with the aircraft continuously in a position from which descent to a landing on the intended runway can be made at a normal rate using normal maneuvers.
12.    Allows, while on the final approach segment, no more than a three-quarter-scale deflection of the CDI or within 10 in case of an RMI, and maintains airspeed within 10 knots.
13.    Maintains the MDA, when reached, within +100 feet (30 meters), -0 feet to the MAP.
14.    Executes the missed approach procedure when the required visual references for the intended runway are not distinctly visible and identifiable at the MAP.
15.    Executes a normal landing from a straight-in or circling approach when instructed by the examiner.

## B. TASK:    PRECISION ILS INSTRUMENT APPROACH (IA, IH, PL, A, AA, HA, PLA, PC)

REFERENCES: 14 CFR parts 61, 91; AC 61-27; IAP; AIM.

**Objective.**    To determine that the applicant:

1.    Exhibits adequate knowledge of the elements of an ILS instrument approach procedure.
2.    Selects and complies with the appropriate ILS instrument approach procedure to be performed.
3.    Establishes two-way communications with ATC, as appropriate to the phase of flight or approach segment, and uses proper radio communications phraseology and technique.
4.    Selects, tunes, identifies, and confirms the operational status of ground and aircraft navigation equipment to be used for the approach procedure.
5.    Complies with all clearances issued by ATC or the examiner.
6.    Advises ATC or examiner anytime the aircraft is unable to comply with a clearance.

7.  Establishes the appropriate aircraft configuration and airspeed, considering turbulence and wind shear, and completes the aircraft checklist items appropriate to the phase of flight.

8.  Maintains, prior to beginning the final approach segment, specified altitude within 100 feet (30 meters), heading or course within 10 , and airspeed within 10 knots.

9.  Applies the necessary adjustments to the published DH and visibility criteria for the aircraft approach category when required, such as

   a.  FDC and Class II NOTAM s.
   b.  inoperative aircraft and ground navigation equipment.
   c.  inoperative visual aids associated with the landing environment.
   d.  National Weather Service (NWS) reporting factors and criteria.

10. Establishes an initial rate of descent at the point where the electronic glide slope is intercepted, which approximates that required for the aircraft to follow the glide slope to DH.

11. Allows, while on the final approach segment, no more than three-quarter-scale deflection of either the localizer or glide slope indications, and maintains the specified airspeed within 10 knots.

12. Avoids descent below the DH before initiating a missed approach procedure or transitioning to a normal landing approach.

13. Initiates immediately the missed approach procedure when, at the DH, the required visual references for the intended runway are not distinctly visible and identifiable.

14. Transitions to a normal landing approach when the aircraft is continuously in a position from which a descent to a landing on the intended runway can be made at a normal rate of descent using normal maneuvers.

## C. TASK: MISSED APPROACH (IA, IH, PL, AA, HA, PLA, PC)

REFERENCES: 14 CFR parts 61, 91; AC 61-27; IAP; AIM.

**Objective.** To determine that the applicant:

1. Exhibits adequate knowledge of the elements related to missed approach procedures associated with standard instrument approaches.
2. Initiates the missed approach promptly by applying power, establishing a climb attitude, and reducing drag in accordance with the aircraft manufacturer's recommendations.
3. Reports to ATC beginning the missed approach procedure.
4. Complies with the published or alternate missed approach procedure.
5. Advises ATC or examiner anytime the aircraft is unable to comply with a clearance, restriction, or climb gradient.
6. Follows the recommended checklist items appropriate to the go-around procedure.
7. Requests, if appropriate, ATC clearance to the alternate airport, clearance limit, or as directed by the examiner.
8. Maintains the recommended airspeed within 10 knots; heading, course, or bearing within 10 ; and altitude(s) within 100 feet (30 meters) during the missed approach procedure.

## D. TASK: CIRCLING APPROACH (IA, A, AA)

REFERENCES: 14 CFR parts 61, 91; AC 61-27; IAP; AIM.

**Objective.** To determine that the applicant:

1. Exhibits adequate knowledge of the elements related to a circling approach procedure.
2. Selects and complies with the appropriate circling approach procedure considering turbulence and wind shear and considering the maneuvering capabilities of the aircraft.
3. Confirms the direction of traffic and adheres to all restrictions and instructions issued by ATC and the examiner.
4. Does not exceed the visibility criteria or descend below the appropriate circling altitude until in a position from which a descent to a normal landing can be made.
5. Maneuvers the aircraft, after reaching the authorized MDA to maintain a flightpath that permits a normal landing on a runway at least 90° from the final approach course.

**E. TASK:   LANDING FROM A STRAIGHT-IN OR CIRCLING
APPROACH (IA, IH, PL, AA, HA, PLA)**

REFERENCES: 14 CFR parts 61, 91; AC 61-27; AIM.

**Objective.**   To determine that the applicant:

1.   Exhibits adequate knowledge of the elements related to the
pilot's responsibilities, and the environmental, operational,
and meteorological factors which affect a landing from a
straight-in or a circling approach.
2.   Transitions at the DH, MDA, or VDP to a visual flight
condition, allowing for safe visual maneuvering and a
normal landing.
3.   Adheres to all ATC (or examiner) advisories, such as
NOTAM s, wind shear, wake turbulence, runway surface,
braking conditions, and other operational considerations.
4.   Completes appropriate checklist items for the pre-landing
and landing phase.
5.   Maintains positive aircraft control throughout the complete
landing maneuver.

# VII. AREA OF OPERATION: EMERGENCY OPERATIONS

## A. TASK: LOSS OF COMMUNICATIONS (IA, IH, PL, A, AA, HA, PLA)

REFERENCES: 14 CFR parts 61, 91; AIM.

**Objective.** To determine that the applicant exhibits adequate knowledge of the elements related to applicable loss of communication procedures to include:

1. Recognizing loss of communication.
2. Continuing to destination according to the flight plan.
3. When to deviate from the flight plan.
4. Timing for beginning an approach at destination.

## B. TASK: ONE ENGINE INOPERATIVE DURING STRAIGHT-AND-LEVEL FLIGHT AND TURNS (MULTIENGINE) (IA, IH, PL, A, AA, HA, PLA, PC)

REFERENCES: 14 CFR part 61; AC 61-21, AC 61-27.

**Objective.** To determine that the applicant:

1. Exhibits adequate knowledge of the procedures used if engine failure occurs during straight-and-level flight and turns while on instruments.
2. Recognizes engine failure simulated by the examiner during straight-and-level flight and turns.
3. Sets all engine controls, reduces drag, and identifies and verifies the inoperative engine.
4. Establishes the best engine-inoperative airspeed and trims the aircraft.
5. Verifies the accomplishment of prescribed checklist procedures for securing the inoperative engine.
6. Establishes and maintains the recommended flight attitude, as necessary, for best performance during straight-and-level and turning flight.
7. Attempts to determine the reason for the engine failure.
8. Monitors all engine control functions and makes necessary adjustments.
9. Maintains the specified altitude within 100 feet (30 meters), (if within the aircraft's capability), airspeed within 10 knots, and the specified heading within 10 .
10. Assesses the aircraft's performance capability and decides an appropriate action to ensure a safe landing.
11. Avoids loss of aircraft control, or attempted flight contrary to the engine-inoperative operating limitations of the aircraft.

## C. TASK:  ONE ENGINE INOPERATIVE—INSTRUMENT APPROACH (MULTIENGINE) (IA, IH, PL, A, AA, HA, PLA, PC)

REFERENCES: 14 CFR part 61; AC 61-21, AC 61-27; IAP.

**Objective.**  To determine that the applicant:

1. Exhibits adequate knowledge of the elements by explaining the procedures used during an instrument approach in a multiengine aircraft with one engine inoperative.

2. Recognizes promptly, engine failure simulated by the examiner.

3. Sets all engine controls, reduces drag, and identifies and verifies the inoperative engine.

4. Establishes the best engine-inoperative airspeed and trims the aircraft.

5. Verifies the accomplishment of prescribed checklist procedures for securing the inoperative engine.

6. Establishes and maintains the recommended flight attitude and configuration for the best performance for all maneuvering necessary for the instrument approach procedures.

7. Attempts to determine the reason for the engine failure.

8. Monitors all engine control functions and makes necessary adjustments.

9. Requests and receives an actual or a simulated ATC clearance for an instrument approach.

10. Follows the actual or a simulated ATC clearance for an instrument approach.

11. Establishes a rate of descent that will ensure arrival at the MDA prior to reaching the MAP with the aircraft continuously in a position from which descent to a landing on the intended runway can be made straight-in or circling.

12. Maintains, where applicable, the specified altitude within 100 feet (30 meters), the airspeed within 10 knots if within the aircraft's capability, and the heading within 10 .

13. Sets the navigation and communication equipment used during the approach and uses the proper communications technique.

14. Avoids loss of aircraft control, or attempted flight contrary to the engine-inoperative operating limitations of the aircraft.

15. Complies with the published criteria for the aircraft approach category when circling.

16. Allows, while on final approach segment, no more than three-quarter-scale deflection of either the localizer or glide slope or GPS indications, or within 10 of the nonprecision final approach course.

17. Completes a safe landing.

**D. TASK:** **LOSS OF GYRO ATTITUDE AND/OR HEADING INDICATORS (IA, IH, PL, AA, HA, PLA, PC)**

REFERENCES: 14 CFR part 61; AC 61-27; IAP.

**Note:** This approach shall count as one of the required nonprecision approaches.

**Objective.** To determine that the applicant:

1. Exhibits adequate knowledge of the elements relating to recognizing if attitude indicator and/or heading indicator is inaccurate or inoperative, and advises ATC or the examiner.
2. Advises ATC or examiner anytime the aircraft is unable to comply with a clearance.
3. Demonstrates a nonprecision instrument approach without gyro attitude and heading indicators using the objectives of the nonprecision approach TASK (AREA OF OPERATION VI, TASK A).

## VIII. AREA OF OPERATION:
### POSTFLIGHT PROCEDURES

TASK:    CHECKING INSTRUMENTS AND EQUIPMENT (IA, IH, PL, A, AA, HA, PLA)

REFERENCES: 14 CFR parts 61, 91.

**Objective.**   To determine that the applicant:

1.    Exhibits adequate knowledge of the elements relating to all instrument and navigation equipment for proper operation.
2.    Notes all flight equipment for proper operation.
3.    Notes all equipment and/or aircraft malfunctions and makes a written record of improper operation or failure of such equipment.

# APPENDIX 1

# TASK VS. SIMULATION DEVICE CREDIT

## Appendix 1 - Levels of Simulation Devices

## TASK VS. SIMULATION DEVICE CREDIT

Examiners conducting the instrument rating practical tests with flight simulation devices should consult appropriate documentation to ensure that the device has been approved for training, testing, or checking. The documentation for each device should reflect that the following activities have occurred:

1. The device must be evaluated, determined to meet the appropriate standards, and assigned the appropriate qualification level by the National Simulator Program Manager. The device must continue to meet qualification standards through continuing evaluations as outlined in the appropriate advisory circular (AC). For airplane flight training devices (FTD's), AC 120-45 (as amended), Airplane Flight Training Device Qualifications, will be used. For simulators, AC 120-40 (as amended), Airplane Simulator Qualification, will be used.

2. The FAA must approve the device for training, testing, and checking the specific flight TASKS listed in this appendix.

3. The device must continue to support the level of student or applicant performance required by this practical test standard.

**NOTE:** Users of the following chart are cautioned that use of the chart alone is incomplete. The description and Objective of each TASK as listed in the body of the practical test standard, including all NOTES, must also be incorporated for accurate simulation device use.

---

## USE OF CHART

**X**    Creditable.

**A**    Creditable if appropriate systems are installed and operating.

**NOTE:**
1.  Use of Level 2 or Level 3 FTD's authorized only for those aircraft not requiring type rating.
2.  For the practical test, at least 50 percent of the maneuvers may be accomplished in an FTD or a simulator unless:
    (a)  each maneuver has been satisfactorily accomplished for an instructor in the appropriate aircraft at least three times, or
    (b)  the applicant has logged at least 1,500 hours of flight time as a pilot.
3.  Standards for and use of Level 1 Flight Training Devices have not been determined.
4.  Postflight procedures means, closing flight plans, checking for discrepancies and malfunctions, and noting them on a log or maintenance form.

*FAA-S-8081-4C*

Appendix 1-1

# APPENDIX 1

**FLIGHT TASK**
**Areas of Operation**

| | FLIGHT SIMULATION DEVICE LEVEL | | | | | | | | | | |
|---|---|---|---|---|---|---|---|---|---|---|---|
| | 1 | 2 | 3 | 4 | 5 | 6 | 7 | A | B | C | D |
| **II. Preflight Procedures** | | | | | | | | | | | |
| C. Instrument Cockpit Check * | — | A | X | A | A | X | X | X | X | X | X |
| **III. Air Traffic Control Clearances and Procedures** | | | | | | | | | | | |
| A. Air Traffic Control Clearances * | — | A | X | A | A | X | X | X | X | X | X |
| B. Departure, En Route and Arrival Clearances * | — | — | X | — | — | X | X | X | X | X | X |
| C. Holding Procedures | — | — | X | — | — | X | X | X | X | X | X |
| **IV. Flight by Reference to Instruments** | | | | | | | | | | | |
| A. Straight-and-Level Flight | — | — | X | — | — | X | X | X | X | X | X |
| B. Changes in Airspeed | — | — | X | — | — | X | X | X | X | X | X |
| C. Constant Airspeed Climbs and Descents | — | — | X | — | — | X | X | X | X | X | X |
| D. Rate Climbs and Descents | — | — | X | — | — | X | X | X | X | X | X |
| E. Timed Turns to Magnetic Headings | — | — | X | — | — | X | X | X | X | X | X |
| F. Steep Turns | — | — | X | — | — | — | X | X | X | X | X |
| G. Unusual Flight Attitudes | — | — | — | — | — | — | X | X | X | X | X |

| Areas of Operation | FLIGHT SIMULATION DEVICE LEVEL | | | | | | | | | | |
|---|---|---|---|---|---|---|---|---|---|---|---|
| | 1 | 2 | 3 | 4 | 5 | 6 | 7 | A | B | C | D |
| **V. Navigation Systems** | | | | | | | | | | | |
| Intercepting and Tracking Course of Navigation Systems and DME ARC'S | — | A | X | — | A | X | X | X | X | X | X |
| **VI. Instrument Approach Procedures** | | | | | | | | | | | |
| A. Nonprecision Approach Procedure (VOR, NDB, GPS, LOC, LDA, SDF), if equipped | — | — | X | — | — | X | X | X | X | X | X |
| B. Precision Approach Procedure (ILS) | — | — | X | — | — | X | X | X | X | X | X |
| C. Missed Approach Procedures | — | — | X | — | — | X | X | X | X | X | X |
| D. Circling Approach Procedures (NA Helicopters) | — | — | — | — | — | — | — | — | — | X | X |
| E. Landing from a Straight-in or Circling Approach | — | — | — | — | — | — | — | — | — | X | X |
| **VII. Emergency Operations (ME) & (SE) ** | | | | | | | | | | | |
| A. Loss of Communications | — | X | X | — | A | X | X | X | X | X | X |
| B. One Engine Inoperative, Straight-and-Level Flight and Turns | — | — | X | — | — | X | X | X | X | X | X |
| C. One Engine Inoperative, Instrument Approach | — | — | — | — | — | — | — | X | X | X | X |
| D. Loss of Gyro Attitude and/or Heading Indicators | — | — | — | — | — | — | X | X | X | X | X |
| **VIII. Postflight Procedures** | | | | | | | | | | | |
| Checking Instruments and Equipment | — | A | X | — | A | X | X | X | X | X | X |

* Aircraft required for those items that cannot be checked using a flight training device or flight simulator.

** Multiengine - Single Engine

FAA-S-8081-4C